70121285

Stress Management on the Go

Techniques for Well Being

A practical guide to stress coping techniques
& strategies for on the go people

Andres L-M Larraz

Order this book online at www.trafford.com
or email orders@trafford.com

Most Trafford titles are also available at major online book retailers.

© Copyright 2011 Andres L-M Larraz.
All rights reserved. No part of this publication may be reproduced, stored in a
retrieval system, or transmitted, in any form or by any means, electronic, mechanical,
photocopying, recording, or otherwise, without the written prior permission of the author.

Book cover design by Carolina Botero
Photography by Andres L-M Larraz
www.stressmanagementonthego.com

Printed in the United States of America.

ISBN: 978-1-4269-5777-2 (sc)

Trafford rev. 05/09/2011

 www.trafford.com

North America & international
toll-free: 1 888 232 4444 (USA & Canada)
phone: 250 383 6864 ♦ fax: 812 355 4082

TO THE ONES I LOVE

Contents

INTRODUCTION

The purpose of this book is to help you understand stress; where it comes from, what is the difference between positive and negative stress, how to identify your own personal tolerance levels of different types of stress, and help you choose and develop your own coping mechanisms to deal with daily stress.

The techniques featured in this guide are designed to lead you into a different realm, one in which you will have the choice of looking at situations from different perspectives and the ability to make the situation yours. We will cover different techniques that can be used to make it easier to relate to situations in a less self-harmful manner, helping to empower you into realizing that you can make a choice.

Stress Management on the Go is a compilation of proven, practical techniques designed for everyday life, for everyday people. Simple, yet powerful, functional and effective ways to help you manage stressful situations.

Stress management is about making decisions that will help you understand that you can make different choices, and filter out those that affect you in negative ways. Changing the way you look at everyday situations and transforming your thoughts from a negative to a positive connotation, will allow you to take control of the moment, therefore attaining a different realm, feeling better about yourself, and those surrounding you.

Stress is a part of everybody's life. From the moment you are born, to the moment you die you are experiencing stress. Stress actually makes the world go around and is a necessary part of our lives. Without a certain amount of stress, not much would happen. The trick is to learn how to determine what your own personal, unique, beneficial dose should be, for an optimum, positive state of balance.

This book will help you recognize the different variable levels of stress that are negative for you and help to decide what techniques can be used to modify your psychological and physical response to the negative stressors. The techniques featured in this book are designed in such a manner, so that people in most walks of life can benefit from using one or more of the coping mechanisms to diminish the negative impact that negative stress causes in their lives. The techniques are of an eclectic nature, borrowed from different schools of thought that are not clearly placeable in any one single field, but an integrated combination of different disciplines.

The definition of stress is very confusing; it usually connotes something very negative that we don't want anything to do with. Let's explore it a little bit further and get to know the inner functioning and the effects of the contributing factors that cause stress in our lives.

The topic of stress is discussed incessantly in innumerable articles of varied social and psychological circles. It is often used as one of the main causative and triggering mechanisms to explain almost anything that goes wrong in our lives. The definition of stress tends to focus on the negative feelings and emotions it produces. Most of the definitions of stress incorporate some physiological and psychological reactions to different actions.

Some people refer to stress to describe many types of everyday situations that are the motivating agents in the cause of stress; work, kids, lack of peace and tranquility, traffic, and even relationships as being plagued by stress. It is also used to describe emotions such as fear, anxiety, tension, worry, besiegement, anger or powerlessness, not being in control.

Although stress carries a negative implication, it is also known by some to be a motivator, and a necessary ingredient in a "get things done" type of situation. Stress can be beneficial if projected correctly. It can be used to channel creativity and can be very useful in completing projects. Let's see how we can make stress our "ally".

STRESS RESEARCH & DEFINITION

The word stress has been used so broadly, and many different definitions have been postulated, that it is very hard to just pick one simple answer to what the definition of stress is. Let's begin with one of the best known pioneering stress research authorities.

Hans Selye, considered by many to be the father of modern stress research, was one of the first to study the physical stress response and created the first working definition of stress. He described it as, "the nonspecific response of the body to any demand, whether it is caused by, or results in, a pleasant or unpleasant condition" (Selye 1936).

He called the reaction nonspecific, due to the fact that he observed different subjects reacting to demands with the same nonspecific physical response. Be it heat, cold, ailment, psychological or physical motivating agents.

His research described the health effects of the short and long-term physical effects of stress throughout the body. Selye theorized that all individuals respond to all types of threatening situations in a similar manner pertaining to health effects of chronic stress, which he called the General Adaptation Syndrome (GAS). Selye theorized that as a response to a threat to physical or emotional well being, the sympathetic nervous system (SNS) arousal is activated. In the early 20th century, Walter Cannon described the activation of SNS as the "fight or flight" response; heart rate and blood pressure increase, hearing and vision become more acute, sweat glands fire, and blood is directed to the muscles in order to prepare for either a fight or a retreat.

Selye also theorized that there is bad stress (distress) and good stress (eustress), and that a similar physiological response occurred in both, being it real or imaginary triggering agents.

In the GAS theory, Selye postulated that three different stages of adaptation are exhibited when the organism is continuously exposed to a stressor; first, fight or flight response is activated (autonomic nervous system immediate response), which he referred to as the "alarm" reaction. As the organism keeps on being exposed to the stressor, some resistance to the stressor will be developed by the organism, which Selye referred to as the second stage, "resistance". Resistance continues until the stressor subsides or the organism is worn down. The third stage, "exhaustion", is reached if the stressor does not subside, which ultimately ends with the organism's death (Selye, 1982).

Selye's work focused on physiological responses, which he theorized mainly by observation of lab experiments with animals. His theories were the foundations to a more comprehensive definition of stress.

Joseph McGrath defined stress as a "substantial imbalance between environmental demand and the response capability of the focal organism" (McGrath 1976). This definition of stress implies that the person's level of stress is directly related to their perceived abilities to deal with that particular stressor. So, it actually does not have to be a real threat, it can be a perceived threat. It is the perception of the situation by the individual and not the situation itself.

Fritz Perls, co-founder of Gestalt Therapy, theorized that the here and now is what is important. How the individual contacts his or her existence at this very moment. Stress is manifested by focusing attention to some uncertain future. Gestalt Therapy techniques concentrate on helping the individual face their fears, therefore allowing them to identify the core of the stressors. It is the tension between the now and the future that causes disharmony in the individual. Perls stated that there exists no difference between good or bad stress. Anytime our thoughts leave the present and travel to the future, stress is created. If it is good stress, we call it motivating stress, if it is negative, we call it debilitating.

A more recent definition of stress by Richard Lazarus is the Transactional Analysis Theory, which emphasizes that external factors are not the main source of stress, but the individuals' perception, resources, and ability to cope with the internal or external factors that induce a negative stress effect. This definition of stress focuses on the result of a transaction between the individual and the environment that is perceived by the individual as taxing his or her resources (Lazarus 1984).

According to this model, it is the individual's coping mechanism that is responsible for allowing the situation to become stressful, or simply being a more or less difficult situation. What matters most, is the interpretation and coping process of the situation. Coping has been defined in this model as a "constantly changing cognitive and behavioral efforts to manage specific external and/or internal demands that are appraised as taxing or exceeding the resources of the person" (Folkman 1986).

So, what is stress? For the purpose of attainment of understanding, we are going to adopt a simple working combination of the models previously featured. Stress is set in motion by some type of prompting or stimulating mechanism, called a stressor. Stress is due to the individuals' reaction to perceived environmental threats including actual and imaginary stressors. It can arise from basically anything that the individual perceives as a stressor. Stressors can be real, such as the death of a loved one, or imaginary, such as a fear of swimming in the ocean because you might get eaten by a shark.

Our stress response is our reaction to stressors which can either be a response of physiological or psychological nature, or many times, a combination of both.

The physiological reaction, "fight or flight response", is our body's primitive, automatic, inborn response that prepares the body to "fight" or "flee" from perceived attacks which could potentially harm or threaten our survival. Our heart beats faster, awareness intensifies, pupils dilate, blood is redirected to the muscles, adrenaline pumps heavy, and we become ready for action should we have to fight or run away very fast.

Psychological response, if negative, is the preoccupation, thoughts, fear or anxiety, about whether the individual can cope with the situation.

Worrying about uncertain future outcomes is one major negative psychological response. What if this or that happens to me? What if I fail? Or really, any other "what if" question. It is the perception and the belief that a situation is beyond the individual's ability to control. As a result, the awareness of the situation is narrowed or diminished, and in most instances, will affect our physical stress response, feelings of anxiety, and helplessness. If we perceive and think of the situation as being positive, which is what we want to accomplish, then we can talk ourselves into a stress diffusion state. I can do it! So what if it does not come out this way! It is not the end of the world! So, we place ourselves in a control situation.

Feelings represent our outlook. How we feel about something and how we talk to ourselves has a huge effect upon how we feel. "Your feelings and thoughts are inextricably intertwined" (Lazarus, 1991).

Our perception of what is stressful and how we handle or cope with the stressors is one of the most important parts of the stress cycle. Coping with stress is simply how we handle stress, and what defense mechanisms we have at our disposal to combat stress sources.

If life gives you lemons, make lemonade

EFFECTS OF STRESS

It is not a simple matter to decipher how stress affects us as individuals due to the fact that we all respond to stress in different ways. The factors that interfere with our coping with stress are quite vast; the way we learned to deal with it by observing our parents and peers, genetic structure, personality, and environmental variables. Our response to stress has a tremendous effect on how stress affects our whole being. Mental and physical health can be severely impaired by allowing negative stress to take a hold of us. Some of the factors that can increase our chances of contracting stress related disorders are:

- Acute anger - constantly allowing ourselves to respond to everyday life events in an angry way.
- Negative outlook on life or being pessimistic - always talking or thinking about what is wrong with the world.
- How we "talk" to ourselves - this sucks, I am right, you are wrong, damn traffic, I can't do this, etc.

Stress contributes to many health related problems. Some of these problems can manifest themselves in a psychological or physical manner, or a combination of both, and can have affects ranging from mild to acute. Let's look at some of the contributing factors of negative stress on our systems.

Nervous System

The nervous system consists of the brain, spinal cord and peripheral nerves that connect the spinal cord to all other parts of the body.

The brain and spinal cord make up the central nervous system. The peripheral nervous system consists of the nervous system structures that are not included in the central nervous system.

The autonomic nervous system consists of the sympathetic and parasympathetic nervous system; the sympathetic mobilizes the body's systems during activity-fight or flight response, the parasympathetic conserves energy and balances all other systems during rest.

The brain is the CEO of the nervous system. The relationship between mental health and stress is a very intricate one, as it engages all of the mechanisms of the stress phases. Stress can contribute to various psychological disorders, including anxiety and depression, which in turn can contribute to more severe psychological disturbances. When the mind is compromised by stress, the body is compromised as well.

Immune System

Stress can be a contributing factor to a decrease in immune response and can make us more vulnerable to getting sick. The immune system includes the lymph nodes and vessels that carry immune cells, the spleen, thymus gland, and bone marrow which produces immune cells, and the immune cells that circulate through our bodies.

Our immune system protects us against disease by identifying and destroying viruses and disease producing cells. Research in immunology has shown that stress related disorders have been linked to lower immune system functioning, and as such, takes us longer to heal.

Cardiovascular System

Research on the relationship between stress and immunology reflect an increased risk of heart disease, artery disease, increased blood pressure, blood chemistry changes (such as high blood cholesterol levels), irregular heartbeat, arterial injury, and blood sugar levels. Stress causes the cardiovascular system to work overtime and therefore has been linked to ill effects on much of the system.

Digestive System

Stress can manifest itself by assaulting the gastrointestinal tract and can cause major problems or exacerbate existing ones. Some of the problems include: inflammatory bowel disease, ulcers, gum disease, nervous stomach and nausea, chronic diarrhea, constipation, and Irritable Bowel Syndrome.

Musculoskeletal System

Muscle tension is a very common symptom of stress, mainly the muscles of the back, neck, jaw, and shoulder. When stressed out, our muscles remain contracted and are unable to relax, so acute muscle tension develops, which in turn restricts the delivery of blood to parts of the system, which tends to irritate the nerves, translating to pain.

TECHNIQUES FOR WELL-BEING & COPING STRATEGIES

WHAT WE THINK
IS WHAT WE ARE

We are continuously talking to ourselves, ruminating on thoughts and having extensive internal conversations about almost everything that is going on in our lives. Our inner dialogue has an extremely potent effect on how we feel about ourselves and others around us, and can alter our stress levels dramatically.

The internal self-talk that goes on in our minds can be either negative or positive. Regrettably, negative self-talk, almost always consists of a self-dialogue that includes troubled thinking. We tell ourselves there is something wrong with us, using statements such as, "I am such an idiot",

"I could have done it a different way", "I can't do anything right", or "I should have done it a different way". At the other extreme, we indulge in negative self-talk about those surrounding us with statements such as, "that person is a moron", "they are making my life impossible", "they made me late", "it's all their fault", and other graver, more negative projecting self-talk. Projecting is a psychological defense mechanism, where the person unconsciously denies his or her own thoughts and emotions, which are then ascribed to other people.

Negative internal dialogue can only steer us towards a negative thought process, which in turn affects our rational thinking; therefore causing a state which leads to negative stress. Very simply put, negativity can only evoke negativity and when we start thinking negatively, allowing ourselves to go with it, it starts a process of centripetal force or internal directed self-destructive behavior. This process becomes centrifugal, outward directed, and we start projecting this negative energy towards everything and everyone that surrounds us. If we allow this process to be ignited, it will continue to run around and around in a vicious circle.

On the other hand, positive self-talk such as, "I know I will do better next time", "I am not that good at this, but I am very good at other things", "even though the situation could be better, I am going to make the best out of it", and other such statements will lead us to a process of thinking which will stimulate our stress coping mechanisms, consequently making us feel good about ourselves and the situations surrounding us.

Most events, situations and circumstances we encounter in our life have no significance of their own. We give them meaning according to our own personal past experiences, beliefs and understanding. Therefore, things, people and events do not have the power to upset us, it is all up to the view we take of them and how we allow them to get to us. We do have control over how we interpret events around us and we do have control over how we can change our perception of what happens around us, allowing us to take control of our emotions.

REFRAMING REALITIES

Scoop up the water & the moon is in your hands; Hold the flowers & your clothes are scented with them.

-Zen saying

Reframing is one of the most powerful coping techniques at our disposal and can be used for almost every situation in life. It is basically a way of changing our perception of events from having a negative connotation to a positive one, therefore making a change in the way we would react towards that event.

By altering the frame of reference and the internal dialogue used to experience a certain event, we can easily step out of the box and look at the situation from a different perspective, thus allowing ourselves to change how we "feel" about the experience.

Reframing techniques form an integral part of Neurolinguistic Programming, which is the systematic study of human performance and how subjective experiences can be simplified and transformed into improved components. In essence, how we think, in combination with our internal dialogue, relate directly to how we feel about ourselves.

Two different types of reframing techniques are associated with the alteration of thought process in a positive fashion: Context reframing and content reframing.

Context Reframing

Context reframing is simply taking a concept that is unpleasant, negative or upsetting to us, and changing the conception of the circumstances being experienced so the situation can point towards a positive outcome. Turning a problem into an opportunity. All we need to do is ask ourselves in what context would a behavior have value. For example, we tell ourselves, "It is such a beautiful, sunny day out, but I'm stuck here doing chores." Context reframing it to, "I'll complete all of the chores I've neglected for a while, and not have to worry about them anymore, and there will be other beautiful days when I can go out." Another example could be, "When I have friends over, they make such a mess." Give it value by reframing it to, "I'm so glad to have friends that come over and visit." Basically, all we need to do is ask ourselves "when" or "where" this type of thinking would be thought of as positive or useful. In context reframing, the meaning of the event is not changed, just the situation in which it could be of some value.

Try taking a situation that makes you stressed and see if by asking yourself when or where this situation would be valuable, can you change the context. Watch as the stress disappears.

Content Reframing

In this type of reframing, all we have to do is change the meaning of the event being experienced. For example, the cup is not half empty, but half full. Perhaps you are getting upset because there is so much traffic and you are going to be late. Content reframe-there is nothing you can really do at this point, traffic happens, it is not the end of the world. So how about you take this time as an opportunity and try a relaxation technique you learned, or go into your internal mental library to visit a past pleasant memory, or simply listen to some chilling tunes. Next time leave a bit earlier, just in case.

Another example could be a situation in which you are annoyed at your significant other for being in such a bad mood. Reframing the content would be to tell yourself that everybody has rough days. They are not upset with you, just the days' events; in a relationship, you are there for your partner as they would be for you.

You are driving and somebody cuts you off. What are you going to do? Get angry, start fuming and maybe flip them off? Perhaps, but no, tell yourself that it is not worth it to get mad, that would only ignite the stress response. Smile, and feel good about taking control. Become aware of the situation at hand. Most times, just becoming aware and looking at yourself and how you are reacting is enough.

Going to the dentist is another situation that you can easily reframe. It can be stressful just thinking about the procedure that you are going to undergo, be it a simple cleaning, or a more complicated one, like a filling or crown. Try to think about the benefits and not the procedure itself; the benefits will far outweigh the procedure. Try and imagine yourself after the procedure.

Ask yourself, "What meaning could I give this situation? What would be the purpose of allowing myself to get annoyed? Who would be the one suffering from being upset?" Feel free to use humor when reframing. Reframe it in such a way where you create an opportunity out of every situation.

Remember, it is not the event that makes you stressed out, but rather how you think about the event that determines how stressed you will allow yourself to become.

The words we use to express our feelings also have a lot to do with the patterns our thought process will follow. For example, we might express our thoughts of something we don't like as "I *hate* being stuck in traffic" – The word *hate* immediately reflects major negativity to our subconscious, and as a result, the feelings to follow are negative. Try reframing the "hate" word to "rather". I would rather be in moving traffic or tone it down to "dislike"- I dislike traffic. This simple reframing will defuse the repercussion of a negative subconscious domino effect, and do wonders as a coping mechanism. By reframing negative words, you are adopting a new perspective. When you use the word hate or other negative words, the only one affected is you.

Using these words in conversations with others, such as "I hate waiting in this restaurant," you are still the only one affected, because most people don't care about what you hate.

Try and become aware of some of your erratic thinking, such as talking to inanimate objects, or people that cannot hear you: like cursing at somebody in another car in front of you who cannot hear you, or to a computer that is malfunctioning. Just becoming conscious of our erratic thinking patterns during many situations is the remedy needed to snap out of the stress effect.

Let's take a situation that annoys us and concentrate on the internal language we might use to describe it. Try to reframe the words we choose and notice how the affect will change. Perhaps you tell yourself that you hate paying bills, by reframing it to "I dislike it, but at least I have the money to pay them." It would be a lot worse if you didn't have the money to pay them, which is another reality of life for many people. For example, every time you say I hate something or other, simply change it to perhaps, dislike or would rather. You will see how fast the negativity disintegrates.

DECOMPRESSION STOP

When the source is deep, the stream is long.

-Zen saying

In the sport of Scuba Diving, every time we go down to a certain pressure, nitrogen is absorbed and accumulated in our systems. If we come up too fast, or stay too long at a certain depth, we can develop what is known as decompression sickness. It is the nitrogen forming into bubbles, which expand upon ascent, causing us to have symptoms such as pain in the joints, paralysis, impaired motor function, unconsciousness, and can even lead to death if not treated. Even when we apply all safety measures and calculate our dives not to be decompression dives, we do "safety stops" at a certain depth before surfacing to de-saturate our body of nitrogen in a manner of prevention.

Every time we immerse our self into any type of situation or event, a certain amount of negative stress can be absorbed into our system. Over prolonged periods of time, this negative stress, if not dealt with correctly through coping mechanisms, is stored deep inside, and through a process of saturation, we start developing a "stresspression disease", which can in turn affect us psychologically and physically.

When trying to come up from these everyday situations, let's say, when we come home from work, or after some type of altercation, the inclusion of some type of unwinding or "decompression-stops" are very useful in managing and reducing the effects. Not one single technique works for everybody, so we have to determine if exercise, relaxation techniques, breathing exercises, a simple walk, or getting together for a glass of wine with friends works best for us. Whatever we choose to do, it is highly recommended to create a segmented period of time to gradually adjust to a different mode, a mode of reset, and always do a safety stop!

SELF RESCUE

Even if we have a cup of cool, clean water sitting right
in front of us, if we don't actually drink it,
it won't slake our thirst.

-Kosho Uchiyama

Self-rescue means we are self-dependent. Only "we" can take care of the situation or event stressing us out. Confidence is achieved in terms of how many coping mechanisms we have at our disposal. Before we can cope with any stress-inducing event, we must believe we can deal with the situation. If we believe in our ability to handle the situation, half of the battle has already been won. As a general rule, the sooner we recognize a stress inducing situation, the easier we will be able to cope with it.

Preventing a stressful situation before it occurs is the most basic self-rescue skill. We can prevent stress from affecting us by thinking ahead and recognizing possible events that normally cause us to feel negatively stressed and prepare for them by being ready to use our coping techniques.

How we cope with a stressful situation when it surfaces, which it will, despite our preparation, recognition and prevention, will significantly affect the impact of the effect. Whether it is minor, or whether we allow the event to transform into a full scale stressful situation, is our decision to make.

Take note, perhaps you might want to make a list of all the situations which you recognize as stress-inducing events. Examples: waiting in a line, having to deal with people you would normally prefer not to deal with, paying bills or cleaning the house. Recognize it, decide on coping mechanisms, and put them into effect.

One way we often self-sabotage our lives and let ourselves become stressed is by unconsciously complaining and whining. We complain about almost everything we can think about. We complain about the weather - too cold, too hot, or too rainy. We complain about our physical condition - too fat, too tired, too out of shape, too old, this or that hurts, etc. We complain about our economic conditions - not enough of this or that. We complain about other's actions, likes, personalities and behaviors, sometimes as a manner of gossiping. We complain about our present state, wishing for something else. We actually complain as a means of communication – communicating our negative internal thought patterns. If you really think about it, you probably spend 50% of your awaken time complaining, either to yourself or to others, mostly about little inconveniences of life.

The way you speak to yourself, directly reflects on how you feel. By communicating this negative self-talk to others, you are often unconsciously asking somebody else to change the situation for you.

Self–rescue means recognizing this erroneous thought pattern, by becoming conscious about the way you communicate with the world around you, and by changing negative thinking processes to positive interactions. The simple realization that you are complaining will often be enough to brain slap yourself into a reactive coping state of de-stress. When someone asks you how you are doing, no matter what, just say "Excellent!" By saying excellent, you will ignite an internal positive thought process. Positive attitude is one very powerful self-rescue technique.

Each head is a world. What you consider negative, other people might consider it otherwise. Remember, if you are having a bad day, it does not mean that everybody else is having a bad day. So, snap out of it and rescue yourself from your negative thoughts. Most everything can be reframed.

STOP, THINK & ACT

Do not take life too seriously.
You will never get out of it alive.

-Elbert Hubbard

When faced with an out of hand situation that is causing us immediate stress and we don't know what to do, a lot of times it is essential for us to do a self intervention by using a technique that will swiftly produce immediate results. "Stop" all activity and take control of our breathing by becoming conscious about it. This procedure will help us calm down and oxygenate our brain. Next, we "Think" about what options we have available at our disposal to deal with the situation. Take your time, and stay relaxed. Then, "Act," use the coping mechanism that you decided to use and take care of the stressful situation.

This technique may sound as if it would take a long time to implement during a stressful situation, but it actually only takes a few moments. By training ourselves to follow these three simple steps and not jumping instinctively into a situation and reacting in a stressful inefficient way, we can avoid stress from escalating any further. Through practice and mentally rehearsing how to respond to situations that normally would stress us, we can learn to use the right type of coping technique and act decisively and calmly when faced with whatever we call stress.

Note, when engaged in a confrontational situation, the best technique is to simply buy time to think, and not respond with a distorted judgment of the situation. Pause, breathe, become comfortable with the silence, think about the situation at hand and act in a non- confrontational, controlled manner. We will simply de-escalate the situation. In other words, reframe the situation.

MEDITATION, MANTRAS & HYPNOSIS

Meditation and hypnosis are both used as coping mechanisms for dealing with stress. Both are excellent techniques that require little time and produce amazing results.

Self-hypnosis is very similar to meditation, except that in hypnosis our purpose is different. To be in an active link with our subconscious mind and facilitate some type of insight or outcome.

During meditation, what we normally want to achieve is a state of mindlessness or stillness so our body and mind can relax. It is a break in thought process normally achieved by concentrating on a meaningless word, such as mantras, breathing patterns, imagery or other similar techniques.

Now, give yourself a present; your own personal secret "Mantra". A word used in some types of meditation to break the thought process and achieve a deep meditative state. For the purpose of this book, we are going to use a mantra that has no intrinsic linguistic or religious value so it acts as a thought-disconnecting device. Write your name on a piece of paper and spell it backwards. This is going to be your own personal mantra. Don't worry about the pronunciation; it is supposed to have no meaning. You can actually change your mantra to whatever you want. Our minds are constantly processing and uniting thoughts so we make sense of the world around us. Even when we are asleep, our minds are not at rest. Mantras have a way of suspending thought processes, therefore giving our mind a much-needed rest. You might want to use this mantra when in a meditative state to break your thought pattern.

MEDITATION

Clouds appear free of care and carefree drift away. But the carefree mind is not to be "found"-To find it, first stop looking around.

-Wang An-Shih

There are multitudes of ways that you can achieve a meditative state. We will be talking about meditation first because it will be the stepping stone that will introduce you to a hypnotic state.

RELAX. Begin by taking several deep, full breaths. Close your eyes and imagine that with each breath you exhale, tension starts to flow out of you. As you inhale, imagine that the air you are breathing is going deep past your lungs to every part of your body. As you exhale, imagine your thoughts and worries flowing out of your body. Do this for five or six breaths.

After a few breaths, start concentrating on your toes and imagine a satisfying white light starting to travel very slowly up your legs and with each breath you take the light is making the tension disappear. Allow the light to travel up your legs making them feel heavy and relaxed. Continue this relaxation process, consenting the light to move up through your thighs, buttocks, lower back and stomach, filling every vein and muscle. Feel the heaviness in your stomach as the tension is released. Allow the filling sensation to continue through every organ in your abdomen. Notice how you are starting to feel more and more relaxed.

Allow the light to continue its journey up your chest and down your arms. Continue up to your neck and your head, letting the light unbend, decompress and unwind everything it touches.

Move your head forwards and backwards and roll it around in circular motions, permitting the light to make the tension disappear. Allow the light to move through your eyes, eyelids, forehead, jaw, and neck. Feel the tension evaporate like a mist moving away. Take a deep satisfying breath, and as you exhale, feel your whole body heavy and relaxed.

Carefully inspect your whole body and look for any tension you might have missed. If you find any place where the tension might still be hanging, concentrate the light on it and allow it to feel warm and soothing. Allow it to evaporate.

When a relaxation state has been reached, you are going to begin repeating your personal mantra in thought, and you might find that you are able to relax even further and deeper. You might want to allow yourself to drift into a complete state of mind and body tranquility and let the sounds and scents around you ease you into a mindful rest. Do not worry if your mind gets flooded with distracting thoughts - this means you are entering into the process. It will get easier.

Keep repeating your mantra until you are ready to come out of the meditation session. For you, this could be anywhere from 5 to 20 minutes. Allow yourself to ease out of it slowly. You might want to suggest to yourself that you are going to feel great for the rest of the day, you are not going to allow anything to upset you, and that you are feeling better and better with every breath you take.

The more you practice this form of meditation the easier and quicker you will be able to achieve a state of meditative tranquility.

Remember, what you are looking for, is a moment of mind and body mini vacation all to yourself.

There is no place to seek the mind; It is like the
footprints of the birds in the sky. –Zen Saying

SELF-HYPNOSIS

The mind is like water: when it's still, there is reflection; when disturbed, no mirror. Muddled by folly & craving, fanned by misleading circumstances, it surges & billows, never stopping for a moment. Looking at it this way, where can you go & not be mistaken! It's like trying to look into a flowing spring to see your own appearance-it never forms.

-Seng Chao

Most everyone has experienced a daydreaming like state in which we are so engrossed in our thoughts, that we don't notice the environment around us, such as noise, people or even time. How many times have you been in your car and arrived at your destination without even noticing how you got there? How many times have you been so absorbed in a good movie, that you forgot you're watching one, or you forget who you were watching the movie with? Yes, that simple, you were under self-hypnosis.

Hypnosis is a state of mind in which we are more open than usual to suggestions. Focus, concentration, and awareness are heightened and suggestions appear to be re-directed towards the subconscious mind where conscious criticism is suppressed. During hypnosis we can control areas of our self that normally are not accessible through our conscious mind. For example, if you try to consciously lower your heart rate or decrease the temperature of your body, it is going to be quite hard. Under hypnosis, you can easily make changes to psychological, physical, and even chemical parts of yourself.

There are hypnotic trance states that are guided by someone else, preferably someone trained in psychology and hypnotherapy, mainly for therapeutic purposes, and then there is self-hypnosis. During self-hypnosis what we want to achieve is some desired result, such as stress relief, relaxation, or reframing our negative thought process. All hypnosis is self-hypnosis. Being under hypnosis is simply being in a state of auto-suggestion. Contrary to misconceptions and popular belief, when under hypnosis, we are always under control. We are the producers, the directors and the actors. During hypnosis, we are conscious of the external world and can react to it if necessary.

Self-hypnosis is easy to learn and the more you practice the better you will get at it. But like everything in life, there are techniques that facilitate the process.

There are many ways of reaching a hypnotic state, but first, you must decide on some basic factors such as when, where, and for how long you are planning to go into this natural occurring state.

Selecting a place where you are going to practice entering into a state of hypnosis is not as difficult as it seems. Anywhere that is quiet and where you can get comfortable, though not too comfortable that you might fall asleep. A chair is a good start. After some practice, you will discover that you can go into a mini trance almost anywhere and you will also learn to use outside sounds and even smells to facilitate entering into the different realm. In the beginning, you should practice whenever you can put half an hour away for yourself, where you know you are not going to be disturbed. Later, you will learn that sometimes you may only need 10 or 15 minutes. Dim the lights, turn the music and cell phones off, and if necessary, tell those around you that you need some time to yourself.

There are numerous things we can achieve through hypnosis, but for the purpose of this book we are going to concentrate on the reduction of stress by developing coping techniques through suggestions into our subconscious mind.

The Penetration Stage

We are going to begin the trance state by allowing our self to go in to a deep relaxation state. You might want to use the relaxation method previously discussed in the meditation segment. It is not necessary to be relaxed to enter into a suggestive state, but for the time being, we are going to concentrate on relaxation techniques to put ourselves under a hypnotic trance. Notice which parts of your body seem tenser so you can work on these particular areas later.

Once you feel you have reached a deep relaxation state and feel comfortable and tranquil, distinctively visualize this feeling of relaxation to yourself and try relating it to a place, a situation, or experience that you can identify with and that makes you feel relaxed. Perhaps it is a sunrise or sunset, or the image of flowing water going down a stream. Imagine yourself perhaps as a bird high in the sky being able to see for miles in every direction.

The most important factor about this relational visualization is to be able to relate the feeling of relaxation to an image that you can use every time you put yourself under this auto suggestive state, so you can induce a rapid relaxation state just by thinking of this image you created. Eventually, if you find yourself beginning to feel stressed, just the act of thinking about this image will incite a post hypnotic cue and produce a state of de-stress.

Visualization, a technique all of its own, is an excellent way to infiltrate suggestions into our subconscious mind. The subconscious and our imagination are tightly intertwined. What we are trying to achieve is reach our subconscious through suggestions. It is safe and very similar to daydreaming. Let your imagination go and allow yourself to create the most vivid and real images that you can. The purpose of these visualizations is to help reduce stress by reaching a state of relaxation response.

During the relaxation response, our heart rate slows down, our muscles relax, our breathing slows, becoming deeper, our blood flow becomes more efficient, and our metabolism slows down and balances itself.

Once you have succeeded in entering a deep relaxation state and relating your relaxation to a visualization, start giving yourself a suggestion that with every breath you take, you feel yourself getting more and more relaxed. Focus on your breathing and take a deep, energizing breath, holding it for as long as you can. Exhale slowly and long, noticing how the tension is released from your body. You might want to give the air you are exhaling a color and the air you take in, a different color. Repeat the deep breaths three times. Then resume a normal, relaxed rate of breathing.

Imagine a road that will lead you to your own special place where you can relax and be yourself.

Perhaps you might want to create a road along your own beautiful, private beach, with fine white sand. Start walking and imagine that with every step you take, you feel more and more relaxed. Once in a while, you look back and see your footprints. With every footprint that you leave behind, also imagine leaving behind one by one, any negative thoughts you may have. Allow any emotional feelings such as anger and anxiety to be left behind with every footstep you take.

Feel free to let your imagination wander from thought to thought. Remember, you are the director and the actor of this visualization. There are no critics. You can change the script in any way you choose. You can add or take away colors, sounds, smells. You can make yourself feel colder or hotter. The important thing is to have fun doing it! Perhaps you want to add some sound, like the sound of the wind or water flowing. Maybe some scents such as wild flowers or the smell of wet sand.

Now, imagine your own personal secret place that you have created. It is your sanctuary where stress does not exist and you can go there anytime you want to chill and recharge your batteries. Use your imagination and make it your own. Waterfalls, mountains, beaches, rivers, whatever you want.

You can spend as much or as little time as you want to in that special place. You will know when you are ready to slowly go back. You might want to imagine your negative feelings going up to the sky as if they were air bubbles and disappearing as they climb up and away.

Before you come out of the trance state, you might want to give yourself a post-hypnotic cue or suggestion that will be activated outside of the state of hypnosis. You might want to suggest to yourself that whenever you feel stressed out, you will remember the bubbles disappearing high in the sky taking your stress away, and you can easily switch from a stressful state to a state of calmness and relaxation.

Surfacing

The transition between being in a hypnotic state, to a regular waking state, is very easy to accomplish and there are numerous ways of doing it. Normally, a twenty-minute session of self-hypnosis is enough time to reach a state of stress de-saturation. Sometimes even a five-minute session will do wonders as well.

An easy way of returning to an awakened state of consciousness is following the same path you used to enter the state of auto-suggestion. When you are ready, after you have given yourself a post hypnotic cue, take one deep breath and hold it for a few seconds. As you exhale, allow yourself to come out by simply telling yourself that at the count of the third exhale you will open your eyes and that you will feel fantastic.

Remember, this is a basic, beginner self-hypnotic technique guide for the purpose of reducing stress. Do not make it into anything more. You will know that you have been in a state of self-hypnosis if your time perception of the duration of the practice is distorted, and if you come out relaxed and your stress has been diminished.

Like the water, take the path of least resistance

BREATH OF LIFE

Breathe in, be one with yourself,
breathe out, be one with the universe.

-ALM

Breathing is something we all take for granted, like so many things in life. Yet it is a very important, powerful, and efficient stress coping technique. Just being aware of our breath helps to calm and center the mind.

As one of our primordial instincts, life starts with the first breath we take and ends with our last. The average human breathes around 1 billion times in a lifetime or around 25,000 times a day. Our system needs to breathe to get oxygen to the blood and organs, and to expel the waste products from our bodies.

There are many ways that one can breathe. But to breathe properly, that is, to engage in a stress coping breathing technique that will quickly break the domino effect of negative stress, we must co-ordinate breathing with movement, mind and body.

The breathing technique that we are going to focus on, for the purpose of a rapid break into the stress response, is a combination of Dan Jun, a Ki breathing technique used in Hapkido, a type of Martial Art, and pranayama breathing, used by Yoga practitioners. It is also a part of training for breath holding world record apneists, or free divers. We are going to refer to this type of breathing as "centered" breathing; a unity of calm and active type of breathing.

To start, we need to understand that the process of breathing includes two main factors to be taken into consideration; ventilation and respiration. Ventilation is the process by which air is moved through the respiratory system in and out of the lungs. Ventilation can be thought of as an automatic physiological function, just as the beating of the heart, controlled by the autonomic nervous system, or it can be altered by our conscious will power. Respiration is the process of the breakdown of oxygen from the air, so that the cells and tissues of our body can use it.

Improper breathing, such as shallow lung breathing, hyperventilating, or unconsciously holding our breath, are very common during moments of stress. This can be detrimental to our well being by clouding our thinking and making us more stressed.

During the stress response, often, the breathing patterns are disrupted from a normal, controlled breathing, to an erratic manner, causing a chemical imbalance in our systems. What we want to achieve through this type of breathing technique is "control". If we can control our breathing, we can begin to control stress by controlling emotion.

One can perform the breathing technique in any posture, and in combination with many types of motions, such as walking or running, sitting or lying down, and even swimming. There are two important rules to a correct stress breaking breathing technique. The first rule is that one has to be conscious and in tune with exhalations and inhalations. The second rule is that the breaths have to be diaphragmatic or belly breaths. Most people breathe solely with their upper chest. This is a factor that can actually increase our stress levels.

Another very important factor to consider is that exhalations are to be considered as important as inhalations. We need to empty our lungs completely, something that lots of people seldom do, to be able to fill them up entirely. If the lungs are not emptied wholly, we are just breathing with part of our lungs.

The easiest way to learn to breathe with your diaphragm is simply to place the palm of your hand on the center of your lower abdomen, right below your belly button, and inhale through your nose until you notice that your belly is pushing against the palm of your hand. Now exhale slowly through your mouth, so that your belly also pushes on your hand. Your diaphragm should be pushing on your hand through inhalations and exhalations. Now you are breathing diaphragmatically. Yes, when inhaling and exhaling, your lower abdomen will seem to be expanding.

To begin, let's practice the technique in a controlled, relaxed manner, while sitting down. Later you will be able to do it in any position and in many circumstances that you did not think possible. Start by inhaling diaphragmatically through your nose and exhaling through your mouth. Allow it to become comfortable and regulated. Try keeping the length of the inhalation and exhalation the same, around five to seven seconds. Take deep, slow breaths that fill your lungs every time you breathe in and exhale to empty your lungs completely. Do this for about ten breaths.

Now that you are becoming comfortable, let's move on to a more advanced type of breathing. Inhale, filling your lower abdomen, hold your breath for five seconds, and concentrate on exhaling two times as long as you inhaled. Don't worry, it becomes easier the more you practice. Now you are breathing in a centered manner. Continue until you feel in control. Do not expect to breathe in this manner all the time. It will take time to establish a new breathing pattern.

This type of breathing can be done in as short as a few breaths to accomplish immediate control of a moment of stress or in longer intervals for deeper relaxation.

Note that at the beginning you might feel a bit dizzy, disoriented or possibly other sensations in the body. This is completely normal while practicing deep breathing techniques. Just slow down, and if necessary continue at another time.

Centered breathing is often combined with body movements. Let's try a simple walking and breathing technique. Make sure you have enough space to walk forward freely for a few steps. Look directly in front of you, but don't focus on anything in particular. Next, inhale deeply, filling your lungs, holding it, and start slowly exhaling as you walk forward. Keep walking until the exhalation ends. Repeat a few times until you feel the stress dissipate.

Breathing in a centered manner is one of the most powerful techniques to deal with stress. When combined with other coping strategies, it's even more powerful. Be conscious of your breathing and feel how quickly you can tame your stress.

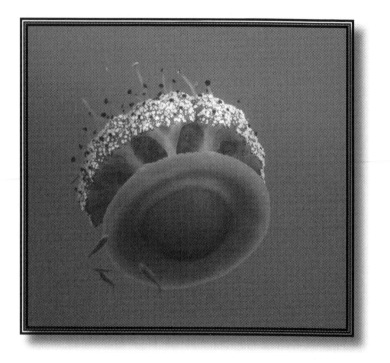

KEEP ON MOVING

When the blade of grass ceases to cast a shadow, & it's not moved by wind or rain, its existence is no more.

-ALM

Mens sana in corpore sano translated from Latin as a healthy mind in a healthy body says it all; mind and body must be exercised together to achieve a state of balance and harmony.

Physical exercise or activity for the purpose of stress management simply means movement with a purpose. The amount of body movement needed to create a great stress coping mechanism is not much and does not have to be strenuous either. It can be performed by most everybody, in most situations and in a relatively short amount of time.

Physical activity and exercise has a tremendous effect on body and mind. Some of the benefits, among many, are: boosting of immune system, prevention of cardiovascular disease, increased energy and self-esteem, weight control, mental calmness, improved mental acuity, reduced anxiety, a better sex life, not to mention a heightened stress coping response.

Any form of exercise is beneficial in dealing with stress. You can do anything that fits your schedule, from taking a walk in between your busy schedule, to starting any of the many available exercise programs or sports activities you enjoy. Put it this way, it's an investment in yourself; the more you invest the better you will feel.

Many types of physical exercise can help reduce stress by activating the production of endorphins, which are the neurotransmitters which resemble opiates in their abilities to create a feeling of well-being. When feeling well about yourself, stress is more manageable.

Some types of exercise that can be performed on the go are:

- Yoga: An excellent exercise that has become very trendy in the western world and is available almost everywhere you go. After initial instruction, yoga can be practiced anywhere and for as long as you desire. Yoga incorporates a combination of stretching, breathing, and meditation techniques, and much more.

- Stretching: This exercise can be done most anywhere and it only requires your willingness to do it and a little know how. You pick the place, the body part and the time. It is excellent for pre-workouts and reduces injury. Stretching is a natural activity that most of us do instinctively even in our sleep. Do not over do it.

- Calisthenics: Deriving its origin from Greco-Roman gymnastics, are a form of simple, yet dynamic exercises designed to increase body strength and flexibility using minimal or no external equipment. When performed in the right manner, can be extremely beneficial to cardiovascular and muscular fitness. You can do squats, push-ups, sit-ups or jumping jacks for example.

- Walking: An exercise that can be done mostly anywhere and requires almost no equipment other than a good pair of shoes. The benefits of walking are often overlooked because many do not consider it exercise. But any aerobic, physical activity, including walking, performed for a total of only two hours per week is beneficial in dealing with stress. A brisk walk for half an hour or walking up and down the stairs a few times a week can be enough. Perhaps you might want to take a walk at night when there is silence and your mind can wander. Try different environments such as hiking trails or the beach. Maybe park a few blocks from where you are going and walk to your destination. You will start seeing a lot of things you might have overlooked if driving or travelling by other forms of motor transportation. If you want to get more out of it, increase your pace of walking.

- Water exercises: Swimming or any type of water related exercises are excellent for mostly everybody at any age due to the low impact level. Water is over eight hundred times denser than air, so you will get a lot more resistance than any exercise performed on land. When you have a chance, try and explore other environments while exercising. Scuba diving and snorkeling are excellent stress management coping techniques that you can enjoy in the ocean, lakes and rivers all year round with the right type of thermal protection.

Whatever you do, just keep on moving! It will keep you younger longer and feeling better and better every day.

EAT TO LIVE

The belly rules the mind.

-Spanish proverb

Eat to live instead of live to eat means something that you already know. We overindulge in our eating habits and sometimes we just live to eat and drink, instead of doing it to feel good.

What we eat and drink plays a very important role in how we feel. Poor nutrition is one of the main contributing factors to major body breakdown. Just to name a few: obesity, high blood pressure, gastrointestinal problems, artery disease and, yes, lowering our stress coping response. Some disorders that are brought about from stress are the results of nutrient deficiencies.

If you are to deal with stress in an effective way, you must feel healthy. Eating well, will make you feel healthier. If you feel well you will deal with stress in an optimum manner.

For stress combating nutrition, simply stay away from saturated fats, and make whole, unprocessed foods part of your diet. Slow down on the alcohol, it might seem like it helps stress, but if abused it actually will become a direct stressor.

Vitamin B complex is a very effective stress combatant. Try juice fasting one day a month and discover a new way to detoxify and clear your mind.

Consciousness and awareness is the answer. You know when you are eating wrong, and what you should be eating. Just become aware and think about it. Stop, breathe, think and act.

The art of being wise is knowing what to overlook.

-William James

FOR LAUGHING
OUT LOUD

Laughter is the shortest distance
between two people.

-Victor Borge

Laughing and smiling are both types of communication that we start using very early in life. A baby will laugh if excited or feeling good as a way of communicating happiness and approval. Laughter is a part of the universal human vocabulary much like crying. Everyone all over the world communicates by smiling, laughing and crying.

A smile usually denotes the emotion of happiness, amusement or pleasure. Smile to help reframe the situation that is causing you to stress.

Smiling helps you keep a positive attitude towards life; even if you are down, try smiling and see what happens - it does not cost anything. Stress easily shows up on our faces. Smile to help change the mood.

Laughter is normally a reaction to some type of stimuli such as a feeling of joy, a tickle or a joke. It is a type of human behavior linked to the parts of the brain that produce catecholamine and endorphins, just like when you exercise, producing a feeling of well being. So we laugh because we feel good and laughter makes you feel good. It is a win-win situation.

Laughing therapy is used as a coping mechanism to treat a variety of physical and psychological issues and has been shown to have short and long term benefits for stress relief. It enhances your breathing rate, stimulates your heart, lungs, and muscles, it raises your heart rate, induces immune function, and increases your stress resistance.

Using humor actively in everyday life, especially about the things that are stressing you out can moderate the effects of negative life events. Try to laugh at the silly things in life. Reframe situations so they have a touch of humor. Change the content or the context of the event, or both.

Start looking at the things that make you laugh and become aware of them. You might want to make note. Hang out with people that make you laugh. Humor is very strange, what makes some people laugh does not cut it for others.

Laugh out loud whenever you have a chance and keep an eye out for a chance to laugh. You can run but you cannot hide. So laugh and smile; laughing and smiling are contagious.

Nothing is left to you at this moment but to have a good laugh.

-Zen saying

Behind a temple was a vine with many squashes growing on it. One day a fight broke out among them, and the squashes split up into angry groups, making a big racket. Hearing the uproar, the head priest went outside, saw the quarreling, and scolded them: "Hey! Squashes! Why are you fighting? Now—everybody do zazen."

The priest taught them how, showing them how to fold their legs and sit up straight, and as the squashes began to follow the priest's instructions, they calmed down and stopped fighting.

"Now," the priest said, "everyone put your hand on top of your head."

When the squashes felt the top of their heads, they found something attached there, which turned out to be the vine that connected them all together.

"What a mistake!" the squashes said, realizing their predicament. "We're actually all tied together, living just one life!" From that moment on the squashes never again fought.

-Zen story

NEUTRALIZATION OF COMPLICATIONS

Complications are basically conditions or situations that can add uncontrollable, complex, or negative repercussions into the equation of life. Life is complicated enough as it is, so let's try to choose the complications that are less stressful.

There is no magical way to eliminate all complications in your life. Not all situations that cause you to feel negatively stressed can be avoided. Nor can every threatening or problematic event that you are faced with be eradicated. By using one or more of the coping mechanisms and techniques reviewed in this book, you can neutralize many of these situations and events. By recognizing the possible negative effects that the situations can cause you, you can make a choice as to how you want to deal with it. By staying in its path, or by simply taking the path of least resistance and neutralizing it, negotiate with it, or eliminate it all together.

To eliminate or neutralize complications from your life, you need to first start thinking positively. Negative internal dialogue causes negative irrational thinking, so look out for the self-sabotage thinking process, and digest your thoughts slowly. Think about how you are thinking. Complaining is a negative thought pattern that can have a domino effect on how the rest of your internal dialogue unfolds.

Neutralize complications by reframing the content, the meaning of the complicating factors and or the context. Allow yourselves to view the situation from a different perspective, and change how you feel about the experience.

Decompress and de-saturate the negativity from your system before it becomes unmanageable. After engaging with complications, take your time to surface.

If you find yourself already sinking into a complicated mudslide, you can always rescue yourself by first stepping back and looking at how you are allowing events to become the complications. Think about how you are going to neutralize the event so you can deal with it. Put your coping mechanisms into action - Stop, breathe, think & act.

Neutralization of complications can be achieved through active stress reducing meditation and visualization coping techniques. You can easily visualize your complications disappearing, like smoke clouds vanishing into the sky.

Complications can be better negotiated with the help of a deep relaxation state achieved through a state of subconscious auto suggestive relaxation technique. Visit your own secret sanctuary to decompress when you need to deal with complications.

Breathe in, be one with yourself, breathe out, allow stress and complications to sway away. Don't forget to breathe! Remember life is not about how many breaths you take, but about the moments that take your breath away.

Move your skeleton and eat wisely. Complications are much better dealt with when the mind, body and spirit are working in unison.

Find the humor in every day's events. Even the most complicated of situations can be reframed into a less stressful condition if you smile while you cope with it.

REFERENCES

Alejandro Chaoul, M. and Cohen, L. (2010). Rethinking Yoga and the Application of Yoga in Modern Medicine. CrossCurrents, 60: 144–167.

Alladin, A. (2008). Cognitive Hypnotherapy in the Management of Depression, in Cognitive Hypnotherapy: An Integrated Approach to the Treatment of Emotional Disorders, John Wiley & Sons, Ltd, Chichester, UK.

Andreas, C. and Andreas, S. (1982). Neuro-linguistic programming: A new technology for training. Performance & Instruction, 21: 37–39.

Bandura, A. (1077). Social learning theory. Englewood Cliffs, NJ: Prentice-Hall.

Bandura, A. (1977). Self-efficacy: Toward a unifying theory of behavior change. Psychological Review, 84,191-215.

Bandura, A. (1978). Reflections on self efficacy. In S. Rachman (Ed.), Advances in behavior research and therapy (Vol. 1). Ocford: Pergamon Press.

Bandura, A. (1982). Self efficacy mechanism in human agency. American Psychologist, 37,122-147.

Bandura, A. (1984). Recycling misconceptions of perceived self-efficacy. Cognitive Therapy and Research, 8, 231-255.

Bates, C. (2011). Lessons from Another World: An Emic Perspective on Concepts Useful to Negotiation Derived from Martial Arts. Negotiation Journal, 27: 95–102.

Bealer, G. (1984). Mind and Anti-Mind: Why Thinking Has No Functional Definition. Midwest Studies In Philosophy, 9: 283–328.

Boone-Heinonen, J., Evenson, K. R., Taber, D. R. and Gordon-Larsen, P. (2009). Walking for prevention of cardiovascular disease in men and women: a systematic review of observational studies. Obesity Reviews, 10: 204–217.

Brown, R. P. and Gerbarg, P. L. (2009). Yoga Breathing, Meditation, and Longevity. Annals of the New York Academy of Sciences, 1172: 54–62.

Brown, R. P. and Gerbarg, P. L. (2009). Yoga Breathing, Meditation, and Longevity. Annals of the New York Academy of Sciences, 1172: 54–62.

Bu, B., Haijun, H., Yong, L., Chaohui, Z., Xiaoyuan, Y. and Singh, M. F. (2010). Effects of martial arts on health status: A systematic review. Journal of Evidence-Based Medicine, 3: 205–219.

Chang, E. C. and Bridewell, W. B. (1998). Irrational beliefs, optimism, pessimism, and psychological distress: A preliminary examination of differential effects in a college population. Journal of Clinical Psychology, 54: 137–142.

Chiesa, A. and Malinowski, P. (2011). Mindfulness-based approaches: are they all the same?. Journal of Clinical Psychology, 67: 404–424.

Chiesa, A., Brambilla, P. and Serretti, A. (2010). Functional neural correlates of mindfulness meditations in comparison with psychotherapy, pharmacotherapy and placebo effect. Is there a link?. Acta Neuropsychiatrica, 22: 104–117.

Henle, M. (1978). Gestalt psychology and Gestalt therapy. Journal of the History of the Behavioral Sciences, 14: 23–32.

Claiborne, J. H. (1972). LAUGHTER AND THEORY OF ACTION. The Southern Journal of Philosophy, 10: 343–352.

Cooper, C. L. and Dewe, P. (2008). The Work of Richard Lazarus, in Stress: A Brief History, Blackwell Publishing Ltd, Oxford, UK.

David, D., Montgomery, G. H., Macavei, B. and Bovbjerg, D. H. (2005). An empirical investigation of Albert Ellis's binary model of distress. Journal of Clinical Psychology, 61: 499–516.

Davis, S. L. R. and Davis, D. I. (1983). NEURO-LINGUISTIC PROGRAMMING™ AND FAMILY THERAPY. Journal of Marital and Family Therapy, 9: 283–291.

Del Monte, M. (1995). Silence and Emptiness in the Service of Healing: Lessons from Meditation. British Journal of Psychotherapy, 11: 368–378.

Ellis, A. (1955). New approaches to psychotherapy techniques. Journal of Clinical Psychology, 11: 207–260.

Epel, E., Daubenmier, J., Moskowitz, J. T., Folkman, S. and Blackburn, E. (2009). Can Meditation Slow Rate of Cellular Aging? Cognitive Stress, Mindfulness, and Telomeres. Annals of the New York Academy of Sciences, 1172: 34–53.

Gordon, M. (2010). Learning to Laugh at Ourselves: Humor, Self-transcendence, and the Cultivation of Moral Virtues. Educational Theory, 60: 735–749.

Gruzelier, J. H. (2000). Redefining hypnosis: theory, methods and integration. Contemporary Hypnosis, 17: 51–70. doi: 10.1002/ch.193.

Halsband, U., Mueller, S., Hinterberger, T. and Strickner, S. (2009). Plasticity changes in the brain in hypnosis and meditation. Contemporary Hypnosis, 26: 194–215.

Hobfoll, S. E. and Walfisch, S. (1986). Stressful events, mastery, and depression: An evaluation of crisis theory. Journal of Community Psychology, 14: 183–195.

Humor - International Journal of Humor Research. Volume 5, Issue 4, Pages 343–356, ISSN (Online) 1613-3722, ISSN (Print) 0933-1719.

Kallio, S. and Revonsuo, A. (2003). Hypnotic phenomena and altered states of consciousness: a multilevel framework of description and explanation. Contemporary Hypnosis, 20: 111–164.

KOPIN, I. J. (1995). Definitions of Stress and Sympathetic Neuronal Responses. Annals of the New York Academy of Sciences, 771: 19–30.

Latack, J. C. and Havlovic, S. J. (1992). Coping with job stress: A conceptual evaluation framework for coping measures. Journal of Organizational Behavior, 13: 479–508.

Laughlin, M. H., Korthuis, R. J., Duncker, D. J. and Bache, R. J. 2011. Control of Blood Flow to Cardiac and Skeletal Muscle During

Exercise. Comprehensive Physiology. 705–769

Lazarus, R. S. and Folkman, S. (1987). Transactional theory and research on emotions and coping. European Journal of Personality, 1: 141–169.

Lazarus, R. S. (2006). Emotions and Interpersonal Relationships: Toward a Person-Centered Conceptualization of Emotions and Coping. Journal of Personality, 74: 9–46.

Lin, Y.-C. and Hong, S. K. (2011). Hyperbaria: Breath-hold Diving. Comprehensive Physiology. 979–995.

Maddux, J. E. and Volkmann, J. (2010). Self-Efficacy, in Handbook of Personality and Self-Regulation (ed R. H. Hoyle), Wiley-Blackwell, Oxford, UK.

Maldonado, J. R. and Spiegel, D. (2008). Hypnosis, in Psychiatry, Third Edition (eds A. Tasman, J. Kay, J. A. Lieberman, M. B. First and M. Maj), John Wiley & Sons, Ltd, Chichester, UK.

McGrath, J. E. (1986). Continuity and Change: Time, Method, and the Study of Social

Issues. Journal of Social Issues, 42: 5–19. doi: 10.1111/j.1540-4560.1986.

McGrath, J. E. and Beehr, T. A. (1990). Time and the stress process: Some temporal issues in the conceptualization and measurement of stress. Stress Medicine, 6: 93–104.

McGuire, W. J. and McGuire, C. V. (1992). Cognitive-versus-affective positivity asymmetries in thought systems. European Journal of Social Psychology, 22: 571–591.

Oei, T. P., Hansen, J. and Miller, S. (1993). The Empirical Status of Irrational Beliefs in Rational Emotive Therapy. Australian Psychologist, 28: 195–200.

O'Neill, L. M., Barnier, A. J. and McConkey, K. (1999). Treating anxiety with self-hypnosis and relaxation. Contemporary Hypnosis, 16: 68–80.

Price, V. A. (1982). What is Type A? A Cognitive Social Learning Model. Journal of Organizational Behavior, 3: 109–129.

Provine, R. R. and Fischer, K. R. (1989). Laughing, Smiling, and Talking: Relation to Sleeping and Social Context in Humans. Ethology, 83: 295–305.

Rosch, P. J. (1998). Reminiscences of Hans Selye and the birth of 'stress'. Stress Medicine, 14: 1–6. doi: 10.1002/(SICI)1099-1700(199801)14:1<1::AID-SMI777>3.0.CO;2-W.

Rosenman, R. H. (1991). Type A behavior pattern and coronary heart disease: The hostility factor? Stress Medicine, 7: 245–253.

Ross, M. H. (1977). Dietary Behavior and Longevity. Nutrition Reviews, 35: 257–265.

Shelton, G., Jones, D. R. and Milsom, W. K. (2010). Control of Breathing in Ectothermic Vertebrates. Comprehensive Physiology. 857–909.

Solomon, A., Arnow, B. A., Gotlib, I. H. and Wind, B. (2003). Individualized measurement of irrational beliefs in remitted depressives. Journal of Clinical Psychology, 59: 439–455.

Vorontsov, A. and Rumyantsev, V. (2008). Propulsive Forces in Swimming, in Biomechanics in Sport: Performance Enhancement and Injury Prevention (ed V. M. Zatsiorsky), Blackwell Science Ltd, Oxford, UK.

Andres L-M Larraz is a licensed psychotherapist in private practice. His specializations include Hypnotherapy and N.L.P. Andres is a Master Scuba Diver trainer, and has 35 years of training in Martial Arts. He has trained Fire, Police & Special Forces personnel in stress management, rescue techniques & martial arts.